ALLOTMENTS

Twigs Way

ALLOTMENTS.

I shouldn't wonder in these days,
To see some haughty misses,
Now allotment gardens are the craze,
Wearing hats trimmed like this is.

SHIRE PUBLICATIONS

Published by Shire Publications Ltd,
PO Box 883, Oxford, OX1 9PL, UK
PO Box 3985, New York, NY 10185-3985, USA
Email: shire@shirebooks.co.uk   www.shirebooks.co.uk

First published 2008.
Transferred to digital print on demand 2015.

Every attempt has been made by the publisher to secure
the appropriate permissions for materials reproduced in
this book. If there has been any oversight we will be happy
to rectify the situation and a written submission should be
made to the Publishers.

A CIP catalogue record for this book is available from the
British Library.

Shire Library no. 469   •   ISBN-13: 978 0 74780 681 3

Twigs Way has asserted her right under the Copyright,
Designs and Patents Act, 1988, to be identified as the
author of this book.

Designed by Ken Vail Graphic Design, Cambridge, UK
Typeset in Perpetua and Gill Sans.
Printed and bound by PrintOnDemand-Worldwide.com,
Peterborough, UK.

COVER IMAGE
Cover design and photography by Peter Ashley. Front
cover: Oxfordshire pumpkin. Back cover detail: Five-a-day
– fresh vegetables in a basket.

TITLE PAGE IMAGE
The popularity of allotments was reflected in postcards
such as this, dating to c.1917. (Amoret Tanner Collection)

CONTENTS PAGE IMAGE
The plotholder's ideal heralded a full dinner plate –
seen here illustrating a book on wartime food
production by Boots the Chemist.

ACKNOWLEDGEMENTS
Illustrations are acknowledged as follows:
Mike Brown Collection: page 20, top left; page 21, top;
page 22, top; page 24, bottom; (Crown Copyright),
page 20, top right. Chatiky Krejcarek.jog, by Petr Vilgus
(2007) from Wikimedia Commons: page 53. Geography,
Journal of the Geographical Association, 60, 3 (1975):
page 29, bottom left; page 31; page 32; page 34, top.
From M. Hall, Allotment Gardening, Ward Lock (1951):
page 28, top; page 28, bottom. Collection of the
Museum of Garden History: page 6 (ref 2002.263);
page 9 (ref 2002.596); page 14, top (ref 1999.481);
page 15, top right (ref 1999.104); page 18 (ref
1999.196); page 19 (ref: 2001.407). Ordnance Survey:
page 4 (first edition Warwickshire XIV.2); page 10 (25
inch first edition Nottinghamshire XXXVIII.14); page
11(first edition Warwickshire XIV.6). Amoret Tanner
Collection: page 12; page 13; page 15, top left.
All other photographs were taken by the author.

Shire Publications is supporting the Woodland Trust, the UK's leading woodland conservation charity, by funding the dedication of trees.

CONTENTS

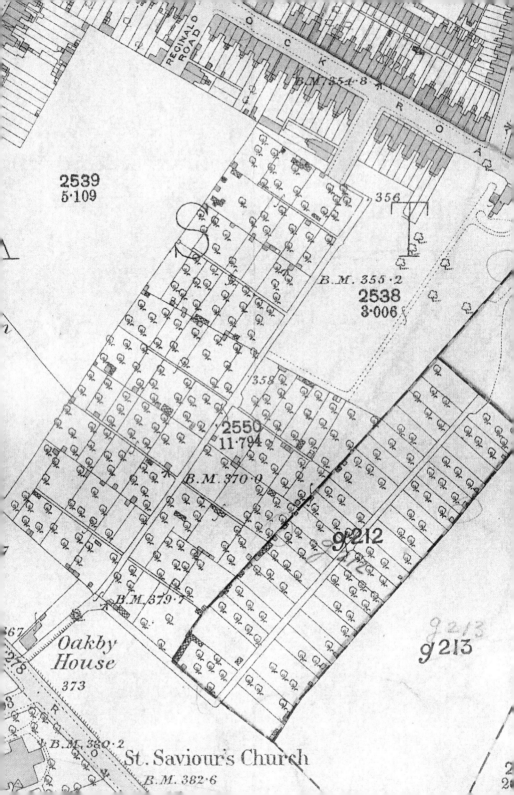

REGINALD ROAD

O C K R O A

B.M. 354·8

2539
5·109

356

B.M. 355·2

2538
3·006

358

2550
11·794

B.M. 370·0

g 212

B.M. 379·7

g 213

g 213

Oakby
House

373

B.M. 380·2

St. Saviour's Church

B.M. 382·6

INTRODUCTION

G IANT LEEKS, tumbledown sheds and doddery old men were the images conjured up by the word 'allotment' for many of the post-war generation. But as the 'baby-boomers' have turned into the allotment holders of the twenty-first century allotments have taken on a new lease of life, a life shaped by modern concerns and modern politics. 'Environment', 'organic' and 'community' are now words more often associated with the allotment than 'war', 'poverty' and 'struggle'. Both the perception and the role of allotments have changed markedly throughout their history. From early years of political strife and association with labour movements through to the victory years of the allotment army and their modern reincarnation as champions of the green cause, allotments have both reflected and reacted to political and social change. As pressure for development threatened increasing numbers of sites, the history of allotments generally, as well as that of specific sites, has become an area of study, and their important role in Britain's social heritage has finally been recognised. Despite change in the role of the allotment, the reality of the 'plot' has remained almost constant since the early days and for much of its history the actual allotment plot has been legally defined as an area 'not exceeding 40 poles [a quarter of an acre] in extent which is wholly or mainly cultivated by the occupier for the production of vegetable or fruit crops for consumption by himself and his family'. How much that definition is the result of political will as much as social need will be seen in this history of the allotment.

Opposite:
On the east side of Birmingham this small patch of allotment or leisure gardens recorded by the Ordnance Survey in the 1890s contains many fruit trees and glasshouses, as well as brick-built sheds or summerhouses.

RULES

OF THE

MIDDLETON COTTAGE GARDENS

1.—The Rent per rood, to be paid in advance, on Lady-day and Michaelma day.

2.—No Garden to be underlet.

3.—No Work to be done on the Lord's Day.

4.—Tenants are required to Cultivate their Gardens properly, and are not allowed trespass, or to damage any of the allotments.

5.—Dogs are not to be taken into the field appropriated to the Gardens.

6.—Tenants are not to have more than half their Gardens in Corn at the same time, n are they to sell any straw off the place.

7.—All cultivation is to be done with the Spade,—the only exception is, that the Tenan may be allowed to plough their allotments once after Harvest.

8.—Either party may put an end to the agreement by giving Three Months' Notice to th other, to expire on the 6th day of April or the 11th day of October in any yea if given by the Landlord, the Tenant to be allowed the value of his crop.

9.—If any of the above Rules are broken, the Landlord may cause the Tenancy to cea at once, without giving any compensation to the Tenant.

I the undersigned HENRY DACRE BLANCHARD, do hereby agree to le and I the undersigned, do hereby agree to rent the plot consisting of One Rood and numbere 29 15 *in Middleton Cottage Gardens, at the yearly rent of* 16/ *and upon the conditions above set forth.*

Dated this 21s *day of* Aug. 815

H D Blanchard

Jabez Witty

Witness,

Robt. G. Callaghan

PLOTS AND POLITICS

EARLY HISTORY

POLITICAL STRUGGLE, social change and class strife scar the early history of the allotment. Although there had been various moves to assert the labourer's right to land since the seventeenth century, the allotment has its official birth in two aspects of social change: the enclosure of the common fields, and the move to the towns.

Enclosure was a centuries-old process by which landholders gained more control over their fields and crops, and by which the labourers lost a wide range of common rights. Although this process had been occurring piecemeal from at least the sixteenth century, during the period 1750–1830 there was an active movement for Parliamentary enclosure by which entire parishes were enclosed in one move, ancient landscapes were divided up with new hedges, and ancient rights were swept away. Spearheaded by the aristocracy and squirearchy, who could rely on local justices of the peace to pass the acts necessary, the enclosures were widely praised by agricultural commentators. However, by the late eighteenth century it was increasingly noted that these changes were detrimental to the rural labourer, and by 1801 even Arthur Young, the pro-enclosure Secretary of the Board of Agriculture, was forced to admit that 'the fact is that by nineteen out of twenty enclosures the poor are injured'.

Social unrest, the bugbear of the landowner and employer, sometimes combined with a genuine philanthropy, gave rise to a number of private initiatives to provide the landless labourer with the means to provide for himself. The most famous of these early movements were the 'cow and cott' schemes promoted from 1765 onwards in the pages of the *Gentleman's Magazine*. Concerned with the high cost of Poor Relief taxation and the wave of crime, advocates of the schemes argued that the availability of land to rent would remedy many of these ills. In 1770, 25 acres (10 hectares) of land was made available to rent by a lord of the manor near Tewkesbury, Gloucestershire, with the result that the Poor Relief taxation was reduced to 4d in the pound, compared to an average of almost ten times that amount in other parishes. Major landholders who supported allotments included Lord

Opposite:
This poster of rules for allotments in 1901 is typical of the period, with no work to be done on the Lord's Day.

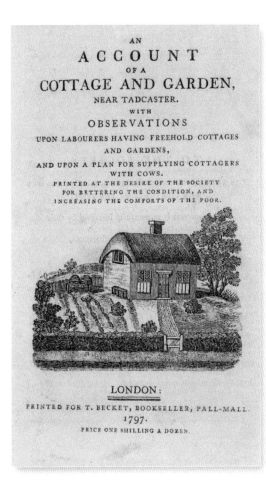

AN

A C C O U N T

OF A

COTTAGE AND GARDEN,

NEAR TADCASTER.

WITH

OBSERVATIONS

UPON LABOURERS HAVING FREEHOLD COTTAGES
AND GARDENS,

AND UPON A PLAN FOR SUPPLYING COTTAGERS
WITH COWS.

PRINTED AT THE DESIRE OF THE SOCIETY
FOR BETTERING THE CONDITION, AND
INCREASING THE COMFORTS OF THE POOR.

LONDON:

PRINTED FOR T. BECKET, BOOKSELLER, PALL-MALL.
1797.

PRICE ONE SHILLING A DOZEN.

This pamphlet was printed by the Society for Bettering the Condition and Increasing the Comforts of the Poor, ardent supporters of the allotment movement and the provision of gardens for the poor.

Egremont on his estates in Yorkshire and Lord Carrington and Lord Scarborough in Lincolnshire, each of whom made land available to rent and in some instances provided cows. Lord Winchilsea reported to the Board of Agriculture in 1796 that the poor labourer in the Midland counties had been particularly hard hit by the loss of common grazing land, and that schemes should also include land where a cow or pig might be kept. Lord Winchilsea was closely associated with the Society for Bettering the Condition and Increasing the Comforts of the Poor, and his estates in Rutland were held up by him as an example of what could be achieved by voluntary provision. A pamphlet extolling the success of another such scheme in the parish of Poppleton, near Tadcaster, Yorkshire, was circulated by Thomas Bernard in 1797. Here the 'gift' of a small cottage (cott) and a rood (a quarter of an acre) of productive garden had transformed the life and livelihood of one of the estate's residents. Transformation was seen frequently as a moral as well as a practical outcome: 'A few roods of land, at a fair rent', wrote a correspondent in the *Annals of Agriculture* in 1796, 'would do a labourer as much good as wages almost doubled: there would not, then, be an idle hand in his family, and the man himself would often go to work in his root yard instead of going to the alehouse.'

These individual initiatives, often associated with the church and usually decried by the less philanthropically minded, were insufficient to guarantee any wholesale relief for the poor or those who had lost common rights. A move to bring in a private member's bill on the provision of land for labourers was rejected in 1790, and the inclusion of a compensatory allotment provision was removed from a General Enclosure Bill in 1796. It was not until 1806 that for the first time an Enclosure Act stipulated that a portion of land should be set aside as allotments; this was the act relating to Great Somerford, Wiltshire, which provided for 8 acres (3.2 hectares), out of 970 acres

(392 hectares) enclosed, to be used as poor gardens at the discretion of the parish. In 1819 the Select Vestries Act gave discretionary empowerment to parish wardens to purchase or lease parish land up to a total of 20 acres (8 hectares) for letting at reasonable rents 'for the promotion of industry among the poor'. By 1831 this was increased to a maximum of 50 acres (20 hectares), which was generally allowed to be let in blocks of up to a quarter of an acre (0.1 hectare). The rural allotment garden had finally arrived.

Its arrival was not, however, universally welcomed. Arguments still raged over the wisdom of allowing waged labourers the opportunity of providing their own subsistence; such worthies as the Bishop of Winchester claimed that granting an acre of waste land to every married labourer would merely result in their becoming 'too saucy', wanting higher wages and breeding more children. Shopkeepers and small market farmers also had a vested interest in keeping the labourer dependent on buying produce. A report of the Poor Law Commission of 1834 summarised the main objection to allotment gardens thus: 'the farmers prefer the labourers should be slaves.' An article in *The Penny Magazine* in 1845 provided an overview of the debate. Where a labourer was paid fair wages and able to purchase vegetables and potatoes from his employer (in the rural farms) or from shopkeepers, no need could be envisaged for the allotment system. Where wages were low and farmers were struggling to provide amongst a superabundance of labour, then allotments might be of temporary use, but even here they would in the longer term encourage immigration of more labourers, give an inducement to early marriage (and thus more children) and generally result in an increased Poor Law burden. In short, the article would admit to benefit only when the allotment was seen as improving the morals rather than the economics of the labourer.

HEATHFIELD CHURCH

Early allotments were often close to the church, as here at Heathfield, Sussex, and many were provided on Church land.

This first edition Ordnance Survey map shows some of the allotments at Hunger Hill, Nottingham. In 1860 three thousand people worked the plots.

Morality was a surprising spur to the gradual acceptance of allotments by the landowning classes. A man with a crop of potatoes to dig, they reasoned, was less likely to spend his time in the alehouse and thus more likely to turn up for work on time. Because too large a crop of potatoes might make him tired, allotment sizes were restricted so that a man would not exhaust himself before arriving at his paid employment. There were exceptions to this preference for small areas of ground: for example, Lord Carrington in Lincolnshire offered 140 of his tenants plots of between 1 and 10 acres (0.4 to 4 hectares), and it was noted that some of these were sufficiently large to set the men up as smallholders.

The lengthy regulations and rules that prospective plotholders often had to agree to reflected this stress on spiritual rather than physical relief. Common amongst these regulations were exhortations to attend a place of worship at least once every Sunday (accompanied by one's family), restrictions on cultivating or picking crops at times when one might be at church, and instant revocation of the agreement if a plotholder was seen attending a public house on the Sabbath day or failed to maintain a moral and sober character. Prospective allotment holders at Tysoe, Warwickshire, were informed in 1887 that 'they must on no account spend too much time and strength on their allotments to the neglect of what was due to their masters, not forgetting that their heavenly master required spiritual work of them on Sundays'. This was despite the resistance of the local rector to the provision of the Tysoe allotments, established by the self-made philanthropist Joseph Ashby.

Numbers of allotment plots are difficult to assess nationally, as was noted by Lord Onslow as long ago as 1886. However, in 1834 there were still probably fewer than 20,000 plots in the country, although these grew steadily to some 100,000 by the 1840s, in part through the hard work and persistence of the Labourers' Friend Society (formed in 1832). Lord Onslow's claim that there were 200,000 plots by 1855 seems excessive and, given his strong political bias against legislation for allotment provision and his argument that landowners were offering sufficient on a voluntary basis, it is possibly an

This 1890s Ordnance Survey map shows allotments on the western edge of Birmingham, surrounded by brickworks.

11

inflated figure. The National Agricultural Labourers' Union (formed in 1872) made the provision of plots one of their primary aims, along with the more ambitious slogan 'three acres and a cow', and numbers of plots were officially recorded as 242,000 (in England) in 1873. Despite the opposition of Lord Onslow, combined agitation by various movements led to the Allotments Act of 1887, which enabled authorities to acquire land specifically for allotments and even compulsorily purchase if necessary.

The Rural Sanitary Authorities were generally slow to act on their new powers: by 1888 over 1,600 acres (648 hectares) had been applied for in total in twenty-nine authorities. None had been granted. Light began to dawn, however, with the county council elections in 1889. These were the first elections since Gladstone's Franchise Act of 1884, and were to become known as the 'Allotment Election', with candidates standing according to their position on allotments. The 'allotment party' won by a small majority and by 1890 there were just over 440,000 allotments, spreading for the first time into the urban areas. In Spalding, Lincolnshire, Halley Stewart stood for the Liberals on the 'allotment ticket' and, having won the seat, retained it for the next seven years. A Local Government Act in 1894 gave further powers for both voluntary and compulsory creation of allotments, while those authorities which were still dragging their heels were addressed by the Smallholding and Allotment Act of 1907, forcing the county councils to become proactive and ascertain what land was required for allotments.

This 1911 Royal Horticultural Society certificate in cottage and allotment gardening demonstrates the interest in allotments at that time, with the recipient gaining ninety-third in the third class!

URBAN ALLOTMENTS
The urban allotment had a rather different history from its rural counterpart. Urban demand for rented gardens had come initially not from the labouring

THE 'LOTMENT
LOVE-LETTER .

I am so MELON-CAULI dear
Since you have BEAN away
The THYME has seemed so
very long
I PINE for you each
day
No SUGAR BEETS your
sweetness - Dont
TURNIP your nose
at me
But take this
18 CARROT
Ring
And LETTUCE
married be.
P.S. A-'LOT-MENT
but not very
MUSH-ROOM

D.mEGi.

The fashion for allotments inspired many postcards on the theme in the early twentieth century. This example is by the celebrated comic artist Donald McGill.

or militant classes but from respectable shop-owners and the skilled working class. Flocking into cities such as Birmingham, Nottingham, Coventry and Sheffield, these newly urbanised 'respectable' classes wanted space to grow their own food, to escape the confines of the city and to share in the nineteenth-century obsession with gardening. As they were able to demonstrate both their morality and their com-parative wealth (in comparison to the farm labourer), landowners were happy to let out areas for them on the edge of the new suburbs, to be subdivided into detached 'town' or 'pleasure' gardens. The annual rent asked for these was relatively high and gave rise to their alternative name of 'guinea gardens'.

Often slightly larger than the 10 pole allotment, these detached (from the house) town gardens were not primarily productive and nor were they as restrictive in their rules and regulations as their rural counterparts. They often combined a lawn and flowerbeds with a small area of vegetables and fruit trees. Brick-built summerhouses, often with elaborate bargeboards, fireplaces and even privies, enabled families to spend their leisure days (and sometimes nights) on the site. Unlike rural allotments, the individual plots were frequently surrounded by hedges and even railings, so that privacy and the idea of a 'garden' were maintained. Their air of permanence and personal decoration made them distinct from the productive allotment. With the spread in Victorian times of middle-class suburban villas, demand for these detached gardens fell, and those that were not built over

13

Urban allotments were less associated with militancy, and their tenants included many skilled and office workers, as portrayed in this 1917 postcard.

The restored Hill Close guinea gardens, Warwick, still display the summerhouses and hedges that marked them out from the more usual 'allotment'.

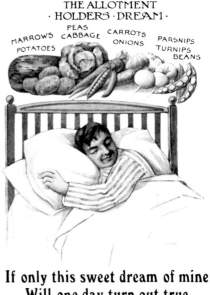

were often converted to 'normal' allotments. Four of the sites that do remain (Edgbaston Guinea Gardens, Birmingham; Hill Close Gardens, Warwick; St Ann's Allotment Town Gardens, Nottingham – the largest and oldest; and the town gardens at Coventry) have been placed on the English Heritage Register of Parks and Gardens of Special Historic Interest, but these are a mere fragment of those that used to surround all growing towns.

As these leisure gardens declined, their place was taken by an increasing number of productive allotments serving the urban poor, who had flocked to the cities in search of work. The Allotment Acts of 1887, 1890 (following the Allotment Election), 1907 and 1908, which had made allotments available to rural workers, also provided for land to be found in the urban areas, and soon vast areas around the edges of sprawling towns were covered in the distinctive patchwork of production that had first marked out their country cousins. As the urban allotment became the new resort for the respectable classes in the early decades of the twentieth century, an 'allotment craze' started, reflected in popular humorous postcards.

Above left:
Joy reigned supreme as all classes caught 'allotmentitis'.

Above right:
A romantic vision from an early allotment holder.

THE ALLOTMENT ARMY

THE INTER-WAR PERIOD

A T the outbreak of the First World War in 1914 there were between 450,000 and 600,000 allotments in England, supplied by a mix of councils, private landowners and the Church. Although the 1908 Small Holdings and Allotments Act had placed a responsibility for allotment provision on county and local councils, there was still an aura of dissent and militancy associated with rural allotment holders in particular. Take-up of new allotments provided under the act had been strongest in the urban areas, where many people had no other gardens, and weakest in the country, where landholders and farmers still had personal power and influence.

The severity of the impact of the war on food supplies was not realised at first, and it was not until 1916 that serious attempts were made to increase the number of allotments available, although from the outset owners of larger private gardens had been urged to donate seeds and stock to existing allotment holders. In December 1916 local authorities were given powers to take over any unoccupied land and turn it into allotments. This move came just in time, as in February 1917 the U-boat blockade of Britain began and the Kaiser threatened to starve the British people into submission. In February 1917 U-boats sank 230 ships and the following month the losses were even greater. Call-up of agricultural workers led to a fall in food production and soon long queues were forming for vegetables, especially potatoes. The blockade and resulting shortages triggered the Cultivations of Land Order (under the Defence of the Realm Act, passed in 1914), which gave powers to local authorities to locate and take over suitable land to plant and harvest as well as ensuring that all allotments were cultivated. By the end of the year there were 1,500,000 plots in active service, producing a staggering two million tons of vegetables. Railway company allotments alone had grown from 27,683 in 1914 to 93,473 in 1918 as those in reserved occupations or too old to fight 'did their bit' on the home front. 'Allotmentitis' swept the country, with postcards and even fashions reflecting the vegetable theme, whilst membership of the Vacant Land Cultivation Society grew to eight thousand.

Opposite:
A Woman and a Westminster Civil Defence Warden spread manure on their allotment in Kensington Gardens in 1942. Behind them is the Albert Memorial. (Imperial War Museum D8334)

Allotments became part of the texture and landscape of national life and were no longer associated exclusively with the labouring classes. Indeed, among the 'short-sleeved army who held the pass with the spade' were women, making their appearance for the first time in the public vegetable gardens. Postcards and photographs of this period show plotholders of either sex, as well as all classes, and even children. Schoolboys at Eton worked plots on the school playing fields, and even girls' schools created allotments for their pupils. Girl Guides set an example by working on public plots, often having to cultivate soil long neglected or under grass. By the end of the war, propaganda, and need, had triumphed and there was an estimated one allotment for every five households. The role of children was emphasised in humorous postcards of the period that showed small girls posed next to large cabbages. The Archbishop of Canterbury even sanctioned work on Sundays, with some going so far as to suggest that church services might take place on allotments so that vegetables and religion might be combined. Allotments became the 'promised land'.

The demand for allotments carried on after the end of the war, and returning ex-servicemen joined the growing waiting lists for plots. In 1919 seven thousand new applicants for plots came forward each week. High prices for vegetables, combined with an increase in urban population and 'leisure time' (with workers being laid off), created a practical demand to match the 'allotment fashion' carefully cultivated by the wartime government. Having established the allotment as a symbol of national and personal pride, not to mention a source of cheap vegetables, it was difficult for the government to turn the tide. But turn it they did, as requisitioned land was returned to its original purpose, often as public recreation areas. Over 50,000 acres (20,000 hectares) were immediately returned to their original uses, despite protestations that echoed the original fight for allotment rights. Some measures were taken to protect the allotment holders, with compensation being offered under the Agricultural Act of 1920 and Allotments Act of 1922.

It was the 1922 act that provided the definition of an allotment that survived for the rest of the twentieth century: an area 'not exceeding 40 poles [a quarter of an acre] in extent which is wholly or mainly cultivated by the occupier for the production of vegetable or fruit crops for consumption by

---

WYMONDHAM

PARISH COUNCIL.

CULTIVATION OF COTTAGE GARDENS AND ALLOTMENTS.

Owners or Occupiers of Cottage Gardens or Allotments in the above Parish, who are unable to cultivate the same, are invited to apply to the Parish Council for advice and help, at the same time giving the reason for non-cultivation.

Persons requiring Plots of land for cultivation should also apply to the above Council.

Applications made under this notice should be sent to the Clerk to the Council at his office in Vicar Street, Wymondham, on or before Monday the 5th March next.

JOHN B. POMEROY,
Clerk to the Council.

WYMONDHAM,
21st February, 1917.

H. G. STONE, PRINTER, WYMONDHAM.

As part of the war effort in the First World War, parish councils ensured that all plots were cultivated and they also managed local provision.

18

himself and his family'. The size and usage were those that had been decided upon as providing sufficient for a family's needs (in the days of large families) but insufficient to encourage attempts at market gardening or profiteering or mere 'recreation'! Until this act allotments had varied in size, with up to 1 acre (0.4 hectares) of arable or 3 acres (1.2 hectares) of pasture, making it difficult to satisfy demand in those areas where land was much sought after and, incidentally, also making the historical assessment of numbers of allotments difficult in areas where only the acreage was reported.

Discouragement and forced removal, combined with theoretical monetary compensation for vacating plots, resulted in the number of allotments falling below a million by 1929, and by the eve of the Second World War to only 819,000. However, although many families gave up their allotment, some did not give up their new hobby of gardening. The inter-war building boom was based on the formula of twelve houses to the acre, which provided sufficient garden space to allow vegetable production without the need for an allotment. In fact, often these houses were provided with gardens that exactly mirrored the size of an allotment. Many of these private middle-class gardens were decorative, but gardening books of the period always recommend a small vegetable plot. For the urban working classes and unemployed, however, such gardens were a distant dream and the lifeline of the allotment again came to be associated with the lower classes during the recession years. Many allotments that survived in the inter-war period were granted new protection as 'statutory allotments' under the 1925 Allotment Act, which laid down that land that had been purchased by councils specifically for allotments could not be sold or used for another purpose without express permission of the Minister of Agriculture.

OUT FOR VICTORY.

THE ALLOTMENT HOLDER.
Too old to fight, but doing his bit to beat the U boats.

This victory postcard was one of several extolling allotments as a means of victory in the First World War.

THE SECOND WORLD WAR

In September 1939 Great Britain declared war on Germany and the Second World War began. Drawing on the experience of twenty-five years earlier, the government immediately proclaimed the humble and discarded allotment as the possible saviour of the country. Within a month of the declaration of war the Minister of Agriculture announced that half a million more allotments would be made available. These were expected to feed two and a half million mouths, making up for the stoppage of food supplies from abroad. Although now widely thought of as the 'Dig for Victory' campaign, the government originally called

Right:
This 'Dig for Victory' leaflet instructed the novice gardener (in this case a woman) how to sow seeds.

Far right:
Allotment holders were continuously urged by the Ministry of Agriculture to feed themselves and others. The usual restrictions on producing food only for one's own family were lifted.

DIG FOR VICTORY LEAFLET
NUMBER 19 (NEW SERIES)

ISSUED BY THE MINISTRY OF AGRICULTURE

it 'The National Grow More Food Campaign' and it was promoted as such by a collection of 'Growmore Bulletins'. It was the newspapers that promoted the rather more strident slogan 'Dig for Victory', which was officially adopted by the government in February 1941.

Promotion and propaganda were almost immediate and by 1942 ten million government leaflets on how to plant, grow, store, cook and even dispose of food had been issued. Not all were focused on the allotment, but its vital role was recognised from the outset with the issuing of a cropping

This woman, shown earthing up celery on an allotment, may have needed instruction in back care!

The best remembered of all the 'Dig for Victory' leaflets. This crop rotation instruction was followed on allotments throughout Britain.

Below:
Cecil Middleton was one of the most popular of wartime gardeners, broadcasting on radio and writing for newspapers and, as here, for Boots the Chemist.

The war-time allotment or back garden

By C. H. MIDDLETON

SPECIALLY WRITTEN FOR

Boots

THE GARDENER'S CHEMIST

plan for a 10 pole plot in late 1939. With immediate provision for again turning unoccupied, waste and recreational land into allotments, the number of plots almost doubled and by 1948 there were an estimated 1,500,000 (the same as at the end of the previous war), although some historians have argued that additional 'private' allotments brought that total nearer to 1.75 million. Many of these adjoined the large housing estates that had been constructed in the inter-war years, and community spirit grew stronger as neighbours dug side by side, tools were lent and seeds shared. Women were again encouraged to brave the mysteries of vegetable growing and many leaflets featured women sowing and harvesting.

Fostering this spirit, the government alighted on the idea of the 'Allotment Army'. The phrase brought a sense of purpose and unity to what was a disparate collection of older men, boys, men in poor health or

THE PLOT

Told Thro' the Sunlight
Window by the makers of
SUNLIGHT SOAP

SHE threw down the hoe and
wiped away the perspiration playing havoc with her very
nice make-up. "Gladys," she
said, "we may be wizards on a
typewriter, but we're not so good
at gardening!"

Gladys and her friend worked
in a government office, and
shared a flat in the suburbs.
When the local council cut up
some grass in the park for allotments they decided they ought
to dig for victory! "There's
the winter to think of, as Lord
Woolton says," said Gladys.

So here they were, on a Saturday afternoon, wrestling with
their vegetable plot.

S 1148-9

Both girls looked enviously at the flourishing
plot near. They eyed the
old man busy on his
allotment. "He looks
grumpy --- couldn't ask
him for advice," they
agreed. And the old man
was thinking, "They look
too uppish to welcome
advice from me!"

But the old man and
Gladys met at the communal water-tap a little
later. She looked at him,
and he at her. "You're
an awfully good gardener,
aren't you?" she said on
impulse. "My friend and
I are duffers at it." And
at that the old man's
heart melted. . . .

"They were right nice
girls after all," he told
his wife that night. "I
gave them a few hints, and
they seemed real grateful."

"What a duck of an old man
he was after all," said Gladys to
her friend over supper. "Isn't
it silly to judge by appearances?"

And Gladys spoke a homely
truth. Life is difficult for a lot
of us one way and another. The
person who seems most aloof is
often the one who most welcomes
and needs a friendly word. So
let's "pool" our friendliness, so
to speak, and see what a difference it makes!

★　★　★

2½d per 8-oz. tablet — 2 coupons

LEVER BROTHERS, PORT SUNLIGHT, LIMITED

Above:
This illustration
originally
accompanied an
advertisement for
Sunlight Soap. It
tells of two female
office workers
who decide to take
on an allotment
and find
neighbourliness
among the
vegetables.

Right:
Laid out on land at
the edge of the
suburbs, wartime
allotments could
be bleak.

in reserved occupations and, by the last years of the war, an increasing number of women. In his foreword to Alec Bristow's 1940 book *How to Run an Allotment*, the Secretary of the National Allotments Society extolled those who 'in response to their country's call, enlist in the Allotment Army'. Certificates of merit were issued to those who made particularly valuable contributions to the war effort by their cultivation of plots, recommendations being made by the allotment societies and local councils. Advertisements aimed at the 'victory gardener' depicted him in a tin helmet and with a fork over his shoulder, like a rifle in the 'shoulder arms' position, and the increasingly frequent parades of auxiliary and volunteer forces sometimes included allotment workers shouldering their 'tools of war'.

Allotments were not confined to the suburban areas, and in the centre of towns public parks and squares were dug up to provide much needed space, with the added advantage of being highly visible and thus a boost to morale. London's Royal Parks such as St James's Park, Hyde Park, Bushy Park and Kensington Gardens, as well many central London squares, sprouted crops. Propaganda photographs were published of allotment holders

From the Minister of Food,
The Rt. Hon. LORD WOOLTON.

"*This is a Food War. Every extra row of vegetables in allotments saves shipping. If we grow more Potatoes we need not import so much Wheat. Carrots and Swedes, which can be stored through the winter, help to replace imported fruit.*

"*We must grow our own Onions. We can no longer import ninety per cent. of them, as we did before the war.*

"*The vegetable garden is also our National Medicine Chest -it yields a large proportion of the vitamins which protect us against infection.*

centre of gravity

Left:
Lord Woolton became a household name as Minister for Food, encouraging the Allotment Army, here in a booklet by the Royal Horticultural Society.

Bottom left:
This 1940s book for the novice allotment holder and gardener was one of the few to feature a female on the cover, despite the increased involvement of women in food production.

Bottom right:
Certificates of merit were awarded to those whose plot was particularly productive.

Above:
Alec Bristow's 1940 *How to Run an Allotment* catered for the complete novice, even detailing what a spade was and how to use it.

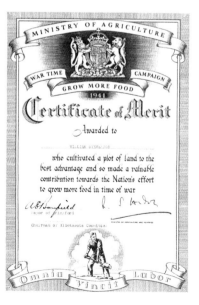

" My Commando son thought he'd help me on the allotment—but it's been too much for him !"

Allotments soon became part of war humour, as seen here in a cartoon by Cyril Bird, known as 'Fougasse', playing on the idea of the allotment as battlefield.

cultivating beside the Albert Memorial. Other locations for high-profile plots included the moat at the Tower of London and a show allotment at Kew Gardens, where regular advice sessions were provided. Training was offered at a variety of local venues, and a series of photographs recorded the Girls Training Corps using the gardens of 145 Piccadilly, the former home of the King and Queen, for digging exercises. Seeds sent from the United States were given to youth groups to create allotments among the bombed sites of the East End, with land permits and tools provided by the Bethnal Green Bombed Sites Association. Photographs of the lads in action were captioned by the Ministry of Information as 'a miracle from heaps of rubble'. Allotment gardens were also created outside Air Raid Precautions posts, so that men would be able to work on their vegetables between watches.

As the war continued, the press joined the battle for the home front and ran columns aimed at the home vegetable gardener and allotment holder. A matter of concern was the inexperience of many of the new allotment holders, and advice often centred on how to use tools, the correct timing of sowing and cropping, and the need to produce year-round crops by thinking ahead. For the first time, the radio, too, played a large part in war, and several programmes were aimed at the productive gardener. Most popular was Cecil Middleton, known as the 'Wireless Gardener' (although he also wrote for the *Daily Express*).

These allotments in the Tower of London moat benefited from being highly visible, and also having rich soil!

He broadcast throughout the war, with an audience of three and a half million tuning in, although his style was said to have bordered on the soporific and so some listeners may have missed parts of his advice after a hard day on their allotments! Even the staff of the BBC adopted an allotment, and a programme called *Radio Allotment* followed its successes and failures through the year.

Crop failures for most people resulted in shortages of some basic foodstuffs. National shortages of potatoes and onions were followed by campaigns for planting, while the more adventurous plotholders were encouraged to experiment with kohlrabi, salsify, celeriac and a range of herbs to enliven increasingly monotonous meals. The introduction of the National Growmore Fertiliser in 1942, 42 pounds (19 kg) of which was made available to each allotment holder, must have spurred renewed optimism at those sites on poor ground. Livestock were also permitted on allotments, with rabbits, hens and even pigs and goats making an appearance, although scarcity of fencing materials could often bring disaster, and rabbits in particular became the province of the 'backyarder'. Pigeons had always been an important element on allotments in the Midlands and north of England, with pigeon lofts dominating many large sites around cities such as Newcastle, but the pigeons were for racing while the wartime livestock was to fill the pot.

Show allotments and roving allotment displays, often accompanied by early versions of the popular radio programme *Gardeners' Question Time* or local 'Dig for Victory' weeks, maintained impetus and enthusiasm, although the later exhortation to 'Dig on for Victory', followed by the 1945 'Dig for Victory Still', hint at flagging imagination on the part of the government. As at the end of the First World War, peace did not at first bring prosperity and food shortages continued. The appalling winter of 1947 caused the loss of many root vegetables in storage (including potatoes) and leek and cabbage harvests froze in the fields, so those who still managed their allotments were afforded some relief from national shortage. But as requisitioned land was again returned to peacetime use, the days of the 'Allotment Army' were numbered as its battlegrounds were taken from it.

Above left:
Contrarily, rabbits might be reared as livestock on an allotment or, as here, could be a pest of the crops.

Above right:
This 1942 advertisement for fertiliser uses a man with a tin hat shouldering a fork to portray the idea of vegetable gardeners as an army.

THE POST-WAR SLUMP

A LTHOUGH VE Day marked the end of the war in Europe, the Allotment Army tried to delay its own 'demob'. As men returned from the front there were extra mouths to feed and more hands to help out, hands that were often otherwise unemployed. The demand for allotments at first remained buoyant, and any spare plots were easily allocated, although in many areas demand outstripped supply. However, the bright vision of the allotment as an heroic endeavour soon started to tarnish and 'grow your own' came to be associated in the nation's mind with wartime austerity. Most of the high-profile 'propaganda' allotments were closed and many of those that were left were in the less attractive areas: at the back of inter-war housing estates, behind gasworks or on railway embankments. Some suburban sites lingered as green pockets in the increasing sprawl, but many more became casualties of the 1950s housing boom.

Another casualty of the post-war period was the female plotholder. Exact numbers of female allotment gardeners during the war are difficult to assess, as even with men away women would often register under their husband's name. However, photographs, propaganda and written accounts give plentiful evidence of women working on the plots in the 1940s. But by the 1950s the wartime spirit of community had largely been replaced by the image of 'men and sheds', and women no longer felt welcome. Martyn Hall, writing in *Allotment Gardening* in 1951, commented that 'whilst some women may make quite a good job of an allotment' many more women were valuable only to 'help their husbands in the lighter tasks of hoeing and weeding'. A put-down for those who had formed the nation's Land Army only a few years previously. A decade later many women were out at work in offices and typing pools, and the sort of liberation offered by a muddy hoe was no longer attractive or necessary.

But what of the next generation of allotment holders? For most of the children who had been press-ganged into endless weeding, collecting leeks in the freezing rain or administering the noxious mixes that turned the humble allotment into a scene of chemical warfare in the 1940s, the

Opposite:
In 1965 it was estimated that one out of every five plots was neglected.

A rare photograph of a woman helping on an allotment, from Hall's 1951 book *Allotment Gardening.*

A typical illustration in Hall's 1951 book on allotments.

Anderson shelters, no longer needed in the garden, were frequently moved on to allotment sites and reused as sheds. This shelter still stands today.

allotment experience was not one they wished to continue. Oral histories recorded decades later often refer to a lifetime aversion to gardening resulting from these wartime experiences. A few went on to garden, and some even 'inherited' the same allotment plot that their father had had. In 2007 a large allotment site in Cambridge had a plotholder who was still cultivating an allotment his father had taken on when it was first laid out in 1939, and other plotholders recalled their fathers, uncles or other relatives working on the site. But those who continued the tradition were the exceptions rather than the rule.

Accompanying the post-war shift in lifestyles was a change in attitude to food. Frozen foods had been developed in the United States between the wars by Clarence Birdseye, and sales began to boom as home freezers reached

Bottom left:
In his 1965 report Thorpe chose to illustrate an Anderson shelter as an example of the hated 'do it yourself' culture.

Bottom right:
In the 1950s and 1960s allotments were most often the preserve of men, frequently of the pre-war generation.

the British market in the 1960s. By the 1970s instant mashed potato was widely available and, in a series of advertisements that exemplified the attitude of the post-war generation to vegetables and home cooking, aliens were portrayed laughing at the ludicrous idea of a home-grown potato. 'Ready-made' became a byword for liberation from the kitchen, and home-made or home-grown produce was only for the poor or eccentric. The humble allotment had no chance against this invasion of modern technologies and attitudes.

By 1947 approximately half a million plots had disappeared, and by 1950 allotment numbers were down to a million plots, with the highest casualties being among the non-statutory sites. Legislation extending the required 'notice to quit' period to twelve months did little to halt the decline. By 1960 there were just over 800,000 plots, while by 1970 the levels of provision had returned to those seen in the 1890s. These low figures disguised the even lower number that were actually being cultivated, and allotment sites became a byword for abandonment and neglect. Vandalism added to the air of urban 'wasteland' as sheds were broken into and glasshouse panes were smashed. Plotholders in Letchworth who complained about vandalism in the 1970s were advised by the district council, as the council was impotent over such matters, that they should form their own vigilante groups.

Concerned that the collections of hastily relocated Anderson shelters, rusting water tanks and weeds did not convey the image of modern, 'swinging' Britain, in 1965 the government decided to review the legislation covering allotments and their provision in the light of current requirements. Modernism and development were obviously on their minds. Professor Harry Thorpe, head of the Department of Geography at the University of Birmingham, was appointed chairman of the committee of inquiry. In an article for the journal of the Geographical Association, written ten years later, Thorpe recalled that the term 'allotment site' conjured up in many people's minds a rather sordid picture of a monotonous grid of rectangular plots, devoted mainly to vegetables and bush fruits and tended by an older stratum of society, particularly men over forty and including many old age pensioners. 'Prominent over many sites were assemblages of ramshackle huts, redolent of "do-it-yourself", from the corrugated iron roofs of which sagging down-spouting carried rainwater into a motley collection of receptacles long since rejected elsewhere... One in five plots lay abandoned... and weeds flourished waist high... valuable land lying derelict.' Some sites even contained a 'sordid selection of livestock'. He presented a sorry picture of the once proud and heroic achievements of the nation's saviours. Allotments, Thorpe announced, were (once again) associated with 'the stink of charity and economic motive'.

Many of the older allotment sites, Thorpe noted, still retained names such as 'Poor's Land', 'Hunger Hills', 'the Doles' or 'Charity Lands', all dating to the pre-war periods of philanthropy and poverty but outdated in the 1960s. Large sites laid out to meet wartime needs were frequently too large for their present population or displayed a distressing association with the working classes, as the

THE IMPROVEMENT OF AN ALLOTMENT GARDEN SITE.
PHASE I: EXISTING LAYOUT.

NOTATION
▬▬ Boundary of site
········ Allotment gardens
▬▬▬ Surfaced road
═══ Other roads / tracks
Turfed areas
Trees (coniferous)
Trees (deciduous / evergreen)
Shrubs / hedges
Community centre
▫ Garden sheds
Water courses
• Water tap

0   100   200   300 feet

Thorpe's plan of a typical allotment garden site, which he contrasted with his proposed new layout.

31

middle classes had retreated to their own sizeable gardens. The solution to this 'problem' as proposed by Thorpe was to reinvent allotments as leisure gardens for the middle classes. Turning back to the idea of the guinea gardens, Thorpe proposed that a selection of sites should be replanned and rejuvenated, whilst

THE IMPROVEMENT OF AN ALLOTMENT GARDEN SITE. PHASE II : DESIGN FOR LEISURE GARDENING.

Thorpe's proposed plan for an allotment site, showing the cul-de-sac layout.

the 'excess' should be released for building on. The 'valuable land' that he had identified was seen as an ideal source for replenishing the government's coffers. Remaining sites would be laid out as attractive plots of varying shapes placed around cul-de-sacs (a favourite of 1960s town planning) and with a central communal building. Individual summerhouses of identical construction would be made available for each plot at a reasonable cost, and families would be encouraged to come and spend the day in their garden.

Flowers and even lawns were to be encouraged and individual parking spaces would be allocated. The last was a clear indication of the class of plotholder that Thorpe was envisaging as in the mid 1960s car ownership was by no means universal. Communal activities, including harvest festivals and Christmas parties, would be encouraged, as would 'open days' when surrounding residents might come in and admire the gardens. No longer cultivated for economic necessity, the sites would be renamed 'leisure gardens' and be associated with rewarding recreation for the middle classes. They would, Thorpe declared, become a status symbol of the leisured classes, something to aspire to rather than a sign of desperation. The new sites were designed to appeal to a 'much broader age, sex and occupational structure' of plotholders, with articulate and organised allotment communities taking pride in the appearance of their sites. In this brave new world the elderly and those unable (or unwilling) to keep their plot to the required standard would have no place. Gone would be the ramshackle sheds, and the ramshackle men who had built them, invited back only on high days and holidays to join in the communal activities in the communal shed.

Under Thorpe's guidance, several of these plots were laid out, in particular the Westwood Heath Leisure Gardens in Coventry, while other sites in Cardiff, Bristol, Portsmouth and Manchester were 'upgraded' with new layouts and sheds. Many of these cities had been at the forefront of leisure gardens in the eighteenth century. Along with the improvement came rises in the rent, both a reflection of the investment in the sites and an

Westwood Heath Leisure Gardens site, Coventry, was one of the 'new' sites designed by Professor Harry Thorpe. These were described as 'higher order' sites.

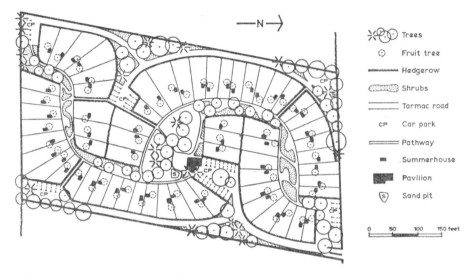

A close-up of the new site at Westwood Heath, showing the numerous trees, hedges and summerhouses. The site had much in common with the eighteenth-century 'guinea gardens'.

BE CERTAIN OF A
VICTORY GARDEN
BY HAVING IN READINESS
ONE OR MORE OF THE
FAMOUS "CORRY" AIDS

CORRY'S WHITE FLY DEATH
CORRY'S SLUG DEATH
CORRY'S LIME SULPHUR WASH
CORRY'S QUASSIA EXTRACT WASH
CORRY'S DERRIS DUSTING POWDER
CORRY'S DERRIS INSECTICIDE
CORRY'S DERRIS LIQUID EXTRACT
CORRY'S NICOTINE POWDER
CORRY'S PYRETHRUM POWDER
CORRY'S ANT AND WOODLICE POWDER
CORRY'S WASP NEST DESTROYER
CORRY'S FRUIT TREE GREASE
CORRY'S CHESHUNT COMPOUND
CORRY'S BORDEAUX MIXTURE
CORRY'S NAPHTHALENE
CORRY'S TENAX GRAFTING WAX
CORRY'S PEPPER DUST
CORRY'S FOWLER'S TOBACCO POWDER
CORRY'S SUMMER CLOUD
CORRY'S RED SPIDER DEATH
CORRY'S WOOLLY APHIS DEATH
CORRY'S RABBIT TREE PROTECTOR

Sold by all Seedsmen and Horticultural Dealers

CORRY & CO., LTD. SHAD THAMES, LONDON S.E.I.

attempt to raise the social status of allotments, again reflecting similarities with the eighteenth-century 'guinea garden'. But before the 'new improved' leisure gardens could sweep the country there was to be a further twist to the allotment tale.

Growing concern about the use of pesticides and their impact on the environment resulted by the 1970s in the establishment of the 'green' movement and a renewed interest in self-sufficiency. Gently satirised in the popular BBC situation comedy *The Good Life* (1975–78), growing your own food was back in fashion and, along with it, so were allotments. Paradoxically, it was the very middle classes that Thorpe had hoped to tempt back with his leisure gardens who were now to invade the allotment plot, but,

This list of instant death for everything from woolly aphis to slugs was typical of gardening manuals of the 1940s and 1950s. The infamous DDT was to be added to this list just after the war.

rather than neat, tidy leisure gardens, they were interested in the very weeds, wildlife and recycling that Thorpe had tried to banish. The rate of decline in allotment numbers slowed, and from 1970 to 1977 only a further 30,000 plots were lost; there was even a surge in waiting-list numbers in certain areas. Friends of the Earth, the environmental group founded in 1971, joined in the fight to retain allotments by publishing *Economic Growth – the Allotments Campaign Guide* in 1979. By the mid 1980s, however, development pressures had mounted and interest in the 'good life' waned. By 1997 the number of plots was down to 265,000, with 44,000 of those being listed as vacant. The outlook was bleak and the history of the allotment appeared to be nearing its conclusion.

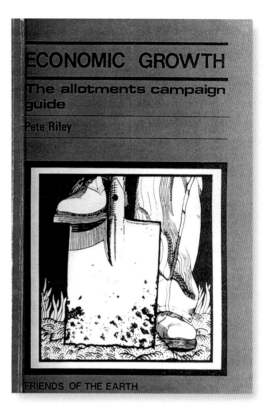

ECONOMIC GROWTH

The allotments campaign guide

Pete Riley

FRIENDS OF THE EARTH

Above:
As an environmental campaign group, Friends of the Earth were keen to encourage allotments.

Following the influence of *The Good Life*, allotments once again housed hens.

A FUTURE FOR ALLOTMENTS?

A S ALLOTMENT numbers sank to their lowest since 1850, the social and political tide was about to turn once again for the plotholder. In the 1990s concern was increasing about the methods by which food was being produced. Added to the herbicide and pesticide scares of the 1970s and 1980s were worries over genetic modification and the 'air miles' flown by out-of-season vegetables appearing on supermarket shelves. Such well-travelled foodstuffs were thought to be substantial contributors to climate change, and local, organic produce became quickly fashionable. Ecological, rather than economic, concerns resulted in an influx of prospective new allotment holders and some returnees, who had first ventured forth in the late 1970s but lapsed in the 1980s. On most sites the newcomers found a core of long-established plotholders sometimes resistant or even expressly hostile to these environmental concerns, but still glad to have an influx of reinforcements to stave off the constant threat of development. Often vocal and used to campaigning, the incomers were concerned to find numbers of sites decreasing, with resultant waiting lists in some urban areas, especially in the south.

Responding to these concerns about loss of allotment sites in both urban and rural areas, the House of Commons Environment, Transport and Regional Affairs Committee produced a report in 1998 entitled *The Future of Allotments*. The committee recorded the lowest level of allotment provision since before the 1887 Allotments Act, with only 250,000 allotment holders, 43,000 plots vacant, and 13,000 people on waiting lists (demand and provision being unequal in different parts of the country). Factors that they identified as influencing this decline included post-war reclaiming of non-statutory allotments, sale of allotment land for redevelopment (in particular housing), apathy amongst local authorities responsible for advertising allotment provision, and the increase in the range of leisure pursuits available to the population in general. Of these, redevelopment pressure was seen by many in the allotment fraternity as the most significant. Sites that were once on the periphery of towns were now well within the urban limits, and their scale and location made them attractive for both residential and commercial

Opposite:
Newly fashionable
they may be, but
some allotments
look just as they
have always done!

Right:
Hollyhocks tower
over allotment
sheds.

development. Financially hard-pressed local authorities found it difficult to argue for the retention of sites when substantial sums could be gained by their sale, or urgently needed homes built. Developers pointed to unoccupied plots as evidence of lack of need, although rumours of development proposals could act as a blight on a site, with prospective and even present plotholders unwilling to put any effort into a plot with an uncertain future. The committee heard of one site that was facing its third planning application in three years. Legislation relating to allotment provision and protection was described as generally confused and often little understood by those who were

Below left:
'Meaning and
beauty with local
distinctiveness'
was the claim of
the report by the
Department for
the Environment,
Transport and the
Regions.

Below right:
Increasing numbers
of flowers on
allotments
encourage wildlife
such as honey bees
and bumble bees.

trying to save their sites, although the National Society of Allotment and Leisure Gardeners (NSALG) gave advice on fighting individual cases. Private sites were, if anything, more at risk than those owned by the local authorities. Railtrack, which owned Britain's newly privatised railway land from 1994 to 2002, explained to the Committee that their policy of redevelopment, disposal or use 'for operational purposes' was expected to result in further reduction of its already heavily reduced numbers of allotments. Church-owned land was also being sold, as funds were urgently needed to bolster crumbling church buildings.

Amid this rather gloomy background of decline, the committee found encouraging signs of new initiatives and strengths of purpose – strengths that would be vital in putting allotments at the heart not only of local communities but also at the heart of government policy. 'Allotments', they suggested, were 'an important feature in the cultural landscape, they combined utility, meaning and beauty with local distinctiveness'. With a positive emphasis on community, diversity, ecology, sustainability, and mental and physical wellbeing, allotments contributed to many government 'targets'. Rather than seeing the aging population on allotments as a problem, the government realised that here was one of the few places where retired members of society could gain fresh air and exercise. The variety of ethnic origins seen on some urban sites, as immigrants squeezed into overcrowded

Above left:
Many allotment holders now practise complementary plantings to keep down pests. Here, for example, nasturtiums are being used to distract black fly from broad beans.

Above right:
Women make up an increasing percentage of plotholders.

Above:
Climate change combined with a greater ethnic mix on allotments has increased the variety of crops grown. Passion fruit and vines can now be seen on allotments in the south of England.

Below:
Uncommon on allotments in the 1940s and 1950s, garlic and sweetcorn are now common crops. In the 1940s garlic was avoided.

housing looked for somewhere to grow their traditional crops, created diverse communities with something to share. The mix of cultivated and un-cultivated plots provided a haven for wildlife, often forming environmental corridors into urban areas and surrounding back gardens. The variation of ecology and the presence of weed species were claimed to provide unique opportunities for birds in particular, but also reptiles, urban foxes, muntjac deer and even badgers.

The report by the Department for the Environment, Transport and the Regions (DETR) alerted many to the way forward if sites were to be saved. Some sites began to work with Wildlife Trusts to promote and enhance this aspect, while others hosted ecological days with local schools and community groups. Even the 'do-it-yourself' so despised by Thorpe was reborn as commendable recycling and reusing of materials, whilst the mountainous compost heaps relieved overstretched landfill capacities.

Government funding and initiatives were combined with the inspiring work on the cultural and heritage role of allotments by academics, as

allotments became a recognised area of study. As Professor of Cultural Geography at Anglia University, David Crouch's commitment to the role of allotments in culture resulted in *Allotments: A Viewers' Guide* (Channel Four, 1992). This was followed by his community programme *The Plot*, which gained a considerable cult following with its insight into the important role played by allotments in the lives of people often on the edges of society. In 1997 David Crouch and Colin Ward published the influential work *The Allotment: Its Landscape and Culture*, which established the social and cultural role of the allotment as a subject worthy of serious study. Reprinted in 1999 and 2004, this became the standard reference work for anyone with an interest in allotments and was referred to in the House of Commons Environment, Transport and Regional Affairs Committee 1998 Report. Subsequent work by this modern-day allotment saviour has included promoting a range of cultural activities on and about allotments, including art exhibitions, community projects, installations and even opera. Emotion, physicality and even sensuality are all aspects of his record of the allotment experience.

More prosaically, an increasing number of government reports and surveys have mapped out possible futures for allotments. In 2001 the Local Government Association published *Growing in the Community, A Good Practice Guide to Management of Allotments*, which recommended working in partnership with community groups. The Allotments Regeneration Initiative (ARI) of 2002 was the result of an £850,000 grant to support the development of models for regenerating underused allotment sites or finding alternative ways of maintaining allotments as public open spaces. The Federation of City Farms and Community Gardens (FCFCG) was awarded a further grant for managing the ARI, underlining the co-operation between community gardens and allotments. Over 2,500 allotment associations and local authorities registered interest in the ARI, and grants were made for projects that promoted allotments outside their normal associations. Schools and youth groups, special needs providers and recent immigrants were all encouraged to explore how allotments might become important to them as the ARI worked closely with groups such as Surestart, the National Health Service and the Probation Service, as well as Wildlife Trusts and Conservation Volunteers.

The Allotments Regeneration Initiative ran until March 2007 and was supported by local and national government. Its legacy was a much higher profile for allotments, combined with clarification of planning policies and publications essential for those seeking to manage sites and gain funding and grants for improvements. It also published a new version of the government's *Plotholders' Guide*, which looked to the future of allotments with an enthusiasm not seen since the 1940s. Regeneration, not only of allotments but of the quality of urban life, was at the heart of this initiative. At Hoxton Manor, London, for example, contact with the local community resulted in a full

The allotments at the new village of Cambourne in Cambridgeshire include a wind turbine.

letting of plots within nine months, with plotholders from Ghana enjoying the opportunity to learn about English vegetables. In Liverpool, out of two thousand plots only 140 were vacant in 2007, and in Birmingham some sites had waiting lists for the first time in decades. Councils have resurrected competitions for 'best-kept allotment site', and in 2007 a plot on the Longbarrow allotment site, Bournemouth, was the *Garden News* 'Britain's Best Kept Allotment'. In 2006 the London Assembly reported that demand was at an all-time high for allotments in London, but that provision was still decreasing owing to building pressure. In 2007 the conflict was highlighted when one of the sites selected for the 2012 Olympic Games endangered the century-old site of Manor House Allotments, originally created by the banker and philanthropist Major Arthur Villiers.

This miniature allotment is for a model railway and is one of many items of allotment ephemera now available.

A variety of 'homes' built to encourage beneficial insects on the new allotments at Cambourne.

New town and 'designed village' developments now include allotment sites, integrated into the landscape by the planners. Cambourne, an entirely new village on the north side of Cambridge, includes an allotment site of some sixty plots with communal compost bins, cycle parking and wind power, as well as a community orchard. A website is used to keep plotholders up to date with news and events, and individual plot blogs can be added to the web. The site was featured in *The Times* when it first opened and was rapidly over-subscribed, with calls for another site to be created. Despite being within a planned village, the site has been laid out on very traditional lines, with rectangular plots running beside straight tracks, and none of the cul-de-sacs or triangular plots as envisaged by Professor Thorpe in the 1960s.

By 2007, although actual allotment numbers were still low (estimated at about 250,000, or one for every fifty households), the profile of allotments

Right:
'Allotment' show
garden at the
Royal Horticultural
Society's Tatton
Park Flower Show.

Below:
In 2007 the
Imperial War
Museum and the
Royal Parks re-
created a 'wartime
allotment' in St
James's Park,
London. An
exhibition in the
nearby Cabinet
War Rooms
accompanied the
allotment.

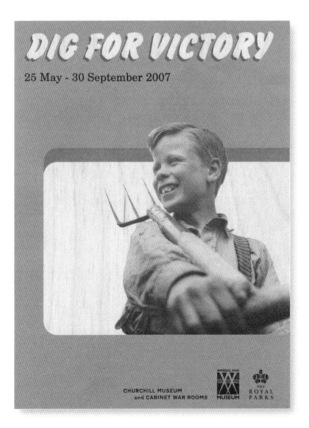

DIG FOR VICTORY

25 May - 30 September 2007

CHURCHILL MUSEUM
and CABINET WAR ROOMS

IMPERIAL WAR MUSEUM

THE ROYAL PARKS

was higher than at any time since the end of the Second World War. The fashion for 'allotment hats' or 'allotment love letters' may not yet have made a reappearance, but the dedicated plotholder can buy 'I love my allotment' jigsaw puzzles, knitted tea cosies on the theme of the allotment (complete with knitted vegetables), miniature allotments to place by a model railway, and T-shirts bearing the slogan 'I'd rather be on my allotment'. A plethora of books advises on how to plant your allotment, how to manage your allotment, how to defend your allotment site, and even how digging an allotment can help with depression. *Allotted Time: Twelve Months, Two Blokes, One Shed and No Idea*, Robin Shelton's story of his recovery from depression, was a surprise book success of 2007, joining the more traditional allotment musings. *Grow Your Own*, a 2006 film about allotment holders challenging development on their site, was released not to a clique audience but to cinemas nationwide, while the prestigious Tatton Park Flower Show featured an allotment as one of the prize-winning gardens in 2005.

It has been estimated that over 20 per cent of plotholders are now women, and on some sites the numbers are much higher. The rapidly falling age profile of plotholders has brought new technology to bear on the allotment. Websites and on-line diaries ('blogs') feature allotments, including such characters as 'soilman', 'welshgirlsallotment' and 'mytinyplot'. In 2007 the National Society of Allotment and Leisure Gardeners marked its 106th year of promoting and protecting allotments with its own website of advice for the new plotholder, and even the *Guardian* newspaper ran an allotment blog.

More practically, allotments and 'guinea gardens' such as St Ann's Gardens in Nottingham and Hill Close Gardens, Warwick, have gained national recognition and protection by being 'listed' as of national historic importance by English Heritage. The Heritage Lottery Fund has also provided funding for projects exploring allotment sites as community heritage, as well as a vital community resource. By recognising the importance of the history of the allotment, we are finally helping to secure its future.

The film *Grow Your Own* was given a national release.

ALLOTMENTS WORLDWIDE

ALTHOUGH the specific history of allotments and allotment provision is different everywhere, the basic idea of the allotment as a small piece of rented garden land is common to many countries, especially in northern Europe. Differences in regulation and appearance are often the result of the specific political and social systems that gave birth to the allotments in that country, some for instance being closer to the idea of the detached leisure garden, others allowing for overnight stays or even longer holidays and giving rise to substantial buildings on the plot. These similarities and differences help to put English allotments into context.

The history of allotments in Germany has parallels with that of the urban allotment in England. Urbanisation of the population in the nineteenth century led to overcrowding and poor living conditions in German cities. Responding to widespread malnutrition, city administrators and employers provided garden areas originally known as 'gardens of the poor'. In 1864 the Schreber Movement was established in the city of Leipzig, Saxony, leasing areas of land for gardens specifically for children to play in and to cultivate, as well as more generally for food production. Although some sites retained their children's gardens into the late nineteenth century, during the First World War emphasis was placed on food production. Immediately after the war, in 1919, the Small Garden and Small-Rent Land Law was passed, providing security in land tenure and fixed leasing fees. During the Second World War Germany did not initially suffer the same sort of isolation as England, but with the increasing destruction of the capital, Berlin, many people moved on to their allotments looking for shelter as well as food. With the collapse of the Nazi regime and failure in food supplies, city dwellers turned to their vegetable gardens. A famous photograph of the period shows Berliners cultivating allotments in front of the ruins of the Reichstag.

With the post-war division of Germany into two states, the *Kleingärten* or *Schrebergärten* developed rather differently in the two parts. In the east the importance of food production resulted in emphasis on the productivity of allotments (also known as *Sozialgärten*). In West Berlin, despite the impact of

Opposite:
An impressively floral allotment near Passau in eastern Bavaria, Germany.

47

Germany's need for food led to allotments being created in the centre of Berlin in the aftermath of the Second World War.

consumerism, the demand for one of these green oases was due not to shortage of food but to the difficulty of travelling to the countryside from this city surrounded by the communist east. The allotments in West Berlin came to resemble the English 'detached town gardens' of the eighteenth century, with lawns and flowerbeds, and even children's play areas. In 2005 there were estimated to be 1.4 million allotment gardens in Germany, with 72,000 Berliners still spending their weekends on their 'second homes', often replete with satellite dishes. Increased pressure on building space has meant that several

In the former East Germany allotments are still objects of pride and the entrances are often decorative.

sites have been sold; the electrical company Siemens sold their site, and German Railways attempted a sale. Support by the Chancellor Gerhard Schröder in 2001 gave some relief to plotholders but government-owned plots are also seen as obvious targets for a bankrupt unified Berlin government.

These *Kleingärten* near Wörlitz in Saxony-Anhalt, Germany, are still fully occupied and immaculately tended.

Unlike English plots, allotments in some parts of Europe are fenced off from each other, with access via a well-kept communal path. This site is near Dresden.

A typical 'dacha' on a site close to the border between the former East Germany and Poland.

A Polish allotment near Krakow. A small summer-house sits proudly by a lawn and flower garden.

Originally founded in 1897 in Grdzioedz, allotments in Poland are known as *Dziaoeka* and the plotholders as *dziaoekowcy*. They rose in popularity before the Second World War and attracted people of all classes. Under the communist regime the *dziaoekowcy* represented a powerful group of citizens, favoured by the regime as an example of urban/rural rapprochement and social equality, and good party workers might be granted an allotment. The allotment would act as a 'reward', allowing them to spend time in their own small dacha, usually a hut made of recycled materials, or sometimes a trailer. Unlike in the United Kingdom and other parts of western Europe, there was no decline in allotments in Poland in the 1960s, and it was only in the post-communist era that allotments have lost their appeal against consumerism.

There are some 960,000 allotment holders in Poland, spread over 5,200 sites, which cover about 44,000 hectares. In common with sites in the United Kingdom, the Polish sites are now under threat as they are frequently in urban areas now regarded as prime commercial land. However, they often have the added complication of being on land in disputed ownership. As the Polish Allotment Federation states, this problem has arisen out of the 'turbulences and system alterations in Poland', when private land was taken over by the state and re-allocated for the municipal good. In the post-communist era some owners are attempting to claim back land that was originally taken from them by the state. Little money is currently available for the creation of new allotments or the restoration of 'dissolved' allotments, but investment is being sought and new legislation passed to encourage allotments once more and the rebirth of the *dziaoekowcy*. Bureaucracy is burdensome, however, with national, local and individual levels of administration and management.

In Sweden allotments have a different origin yet again. Not founded until the end of the nineteenth century, they were inspired not so much by poverty and malnutrition, but for the promotion of family values. According to Anna Lindhagen, the social democrat who was instrumental in their founding, the

Paths and beds on another Polish allotment. Mature trees are common on these sites but banned on British allotments.

Irrigation is key to allotments in parts of Spain.

sites would act as a uniting bond for the family, a place where 'all family members can meet in shared work and leisure. The family father, tired with the cramped space at home, may rejoice in taking care of his family in the open air, and feel responsible if the little plot of earth bestows a very special interest upon life.' These aims were satisfied most frequently not by private philanthropists or the church but by local authorities, and the first allotment site in Sweden was established in Malmö in 1895, followed by a site in Stockholm in 1904. The Swedish Federation of Leisure Gardening was founded in 1921 and still exists to co-ordinate and support the 275 local societies of *Koloniträdgård* or *Kolonilott*.

Allotment gardens in Switzerland also reflect this emphasis on the family, with gardens being called *Familiengärten* or *jardins familiaux*. Again, these were expanded during the Second World War, when the Wahlen Plan ensured that potatoes and other vegetables were planted in all municipal gardens and parks, and the number of allotments also grew, so that Switzerland became self-sufficient in vegetables. Subsequently the tradition continued and has been given a new lease of life with interest from immigrants in the industrial centres such as Yverdon.

Outside western Europe, although the renting of small areas of land for growing vegetables on is often known, the origins, conditions and organisation vary to such an extent that it can be difficult to assess whether they are in the tradition of the allotment. Some countries have larger areas, promoting small-scale market gardening; in some the system is entirely in the hands of private landowners and the rental market. However, allotments on the western European model have been introduced to countries where there was previously no tradition of these. In Georgia for example, large-scale industrialisation and enforced mass population movements during the Soviet era resulted in the creation of new cities with little connection to the rural hinterland. The collapse of the regime and high unemployment have led to severe hardship in towns such as Rustavi, where between 40 and 80 per cent are unemployed. The introduction of allotments on the Swiss model, on land owned by municipal authorities, proved successful, after initial difficulties, and is now spreading to other areas of the Caucasus.

Further afield, allotments were introduced into the Philippines in 2003, when a scheme was set up to provide fifty-five poor urban families with plots for vegetable growing on municipal land that was lying idle. The aims and regulations on these sites differ from the traditional 'allotment' in that produce may be sold to supplement the family's income, an important factor in the success of the scheme. Plotholders also noted that the gardens are strengthening social ties, helping them spend time with their family, and leading to healthier lifestyles with fresh food and exercise. Tax incentives are now being considered for private landowners who give up land for allotment gardens.

Variations on allotments, and on the term 'allotment garden', spread across Denmark, Germany, the Czech Republic, Finland, France, Italy, Poland, Norway, Russia, Slovenia, Spain, Sweden, Switzerland and even Japan and now the Philippines. Most have their origins in the desire to create opportunities for social betterment. Whether it be satisfying basic needs of nutrition and health, or 'engineering' social aspirations or community values, all are related in some way to the struggle for the right to cultivate a piece of land.

A substantial summerhouse on an allotment near Prague in the Czech Republic.

FURTHER READING

Andrews, S. *The Allotment Handbook: A Guide to Promoting and Protecting Your Site.* Eco-Logic Books, 2005.

Bellows, A. 'One hundred years of allotment gardens in Poland', in *Food and Foodways*, 12, 4 (January 2004), pages 247–76.

Brown, J., and Osborne, A. 'We shall have very great pleasure: nineteenth-century detached leisure gardens in west Cambridge', in *Garden History*, 31, 1 (2003), pages 95–108.

Buchardt, J. *The Allotment Movement in England 1793–1873.* Royal Historical Society/Boydell Press, 2002.

Clevely, A. M. *The Allotment Book.* Collins, 2006.

Crouch, D. *The Art of Allotment: Culture and Cultivation.* Five Leaves Publications, 2001.

Crouch, D., and Ward, C. *The Allotment: Its Landscape and Culture.* Five Leaves Publications, 1997.

Garner, J. F., and Clayden, P. *The Law of Allotments.* Shaw & Sons, fifth edition 2002.

Hall, M. *Allotment Gardening.* Ward Lock, 1951.

Holmer, R. J., and Drescher, A. W. 'Empowering urban poor communities through integrated vegetable production in allotment gardens: the case of Cagayan de Oro city, Philippines', paper accessed on-line: www.cityfarmer.org/CagayandeOro.html

Hyde, M. *City Fields, Country Gardens: Allotment Essays.* Five Leaves Publishing, 1998.

Johnson, K. *Gardeners' City: A History of the Letchworth Allotments and Horticultural Association 1906–1996.* LAHA, 1996.

Osborne, V. *Digger's Diary: Tales from the Allotment.* Aurum Press, 2007.

Poole, S. *The Allotment Chronicles: A Social History of Allotment Gardening.* Silverlink Publishing, 2006.

Riley, P. *Economic Growth: The Allotments Campaign Guide.* Friends of the Earth, 1971.

Shelton, R. *Allotted Time: Twelve Months, Two Blokes, One Shed, No Idea.* Sidgwick & Jackson, 2006.

Thompson, D., *et al. Norfolk Allotments: The Plot So Far.* Norfolk Recorders, 2007.

Thorpe, H. 'The homely allotment: from rural dole to urban amenity: a neglected aspect of urban land use', in *Geography*, 60, 3, 268 (July 1975), pages 169–83.

Transport and Regional Affairs Committee, Environment. 'The future for allotments: minutes of evidence, Tuesday 24th February 1998' – Local

Government Association, Allotments 2000 (House of Commons
Papers). HMSO.
Transport and Regional Affairs Committee, Environment. 'The future for
allotments: the Government's response to the report'. HMSO, 1998.
Way, T. *The Wartime Garden*. Sutton Publishing, 2008 (forthcoming).
Wilkinson, J. F. 'Pages in the history of allotments', in *The Contemporary
Review*, LXV (January–June 1894), pages 532–44.

ORGANISATIONS

Cambourne Allotments
Website: www.cambourneallotment.org
Longbarrow Allotments, Bournemouth
Website: www.longbarrow.co.uk
National Allotment Gardens Trust (NAGT), PO Box 1448, Marston,
Oxford OX3 3AY. Telephone: 01752 363379.
Website: www.nagtrust.org
National Society of Allotment and Leisure Gardeners Ltd (NSALG)
O'Dell House, Hunters Road, Corby, Northamptonshire NN17 5JE.
Telephone: 01536 266576. Fax: 01536 264509.
Email: natsoc@nsalg.org.uk
Website: www.nsalg.org.uk
St Ann's Allotments, Nottingham.
Website: www.staa-allotments.org.uk
Wikipedia article on allotment gardening round the world:
http://en.wikipedia.org/wiki/Allotment_(gardening)

INDEX

Page numbers in italic refer to illustrations